A Common Man's Guide to Loving Women

ANDREW MOODIE

A Common Man's Guide to Loving Women
first published 1999 by
Scirocco Drama
An imprint of J. Gordon Shillingford Publishing Inc.
© 1999 Andrew Moodie

Scirocco Drama Editor: Dave Carley
Cover design by Terry Gallagher/Doowah Design Inc.
Author Photo by Sheilagh Corbett
Printed and bound in Canada

Published with the financial assistance of The Canada Council for the Arts
and the Manitoba Arts Council.

All rights reserved. No part of this book may be reproduced, for any reason, by any means, without the permission of the publisher. This play is fully protected under the copyright laws of Canada and all other countries of the Copyright Union and is subject to royalty. Changes to the text are expressly forbidden without written consent of the author. Rights to produce, film, record in whole or in part, in any medium or in any language, by any group amateur or professional, are retained by the author.
Production inquiries should be addressed to:
Playwrights Union of Canada
54 Wolseley Street, 2nd Floor, Toronto, ON M5T 1A5

Canadian Cataloguing in Publication Data

Moodie, Andrew, 1967-
    A common man's guide to loving women

A play.
ISBN 1-896239-46-3
    I. Title.
PS8576.O558C64 1999   C812'.54   C99-900151-5
PR9199.3.M613C64 1999

Dedicated to Harold Alonso Moodie, my Dad

Player's Manifesto (Part II)

Acting is the art of behavioural signifiers. A actor uses human behaviour to communicate information. This information could be based on text prepared for the actor by a playwright, it could be text improvised and set down by a troupe of actors, it could be textless movement, based on the inspiration of a director or choreographer. Regardless what the basis for that information is, the actor is expected to perform behaviour that signifies the meaning of that original impulse. The foundation of all behavioural signifiers on the stage consists of a) performing and action, b) reacting to an action being performed. The number and nature of actions we perform to and react to are infinite. Pick any verb and you will peer into our collective history on this planet: loving, killing, singing, eating, networking, e-mailing. Our actions and reactions are performed in the world, a world that we perceive with our senses. Human beings use their six senses to perceive the world around them—sight sound, smell, touch, taste, and gyroscopic sense (sensing one's position relative to the centre of the earth). We use these senses to perceive things in the physical world, a world which consists of matter of some kind, be it gas or solid, liquid or energy (fire, electricity, etc.). Then there are those things that exist but not as matter, entities just beyond our senses' perception: love, hatred, envy, justice, evil. These are things that we know with our minds, feel with our hearts, sense with our souls.

Actors behave. This behaviour signifies. It signifies that which the behaviour is meant to represent, that which is being signified. I call this the immutable. The immutable is the core of all that is signified. It is the thing itself. The thing that cannot be reduced, the eternal that the signifier is the label, the herald, the harbinger of. Playwrights use text, printed on a piece of paper, with dialogue and stage directions. They do this to instruct the actor in how to build the behaviour of the character they will be performing. All the behaviour of all the characters communicate the play. Playwrights work very hard, weaving a tapestry of human behaviour, a rhythm of signification, its pace and its intensity rising, creating a kind of combustion where the world that we know from our senses, the material world, and the world that we feel with our souls, the immaterial world, combine into one, and for a brief moment in time the immutable exists among us. The force and intensity of this fusion plays upon the actor much in the same way a tree reveals to us the awesome power of the wind. What the playwright needs from the actor is a fidelity to the text, an understanding of the behaviour, a strong, passionate rendering of its signification, and finally, a willingness to become vulnerable to that world of those unseen things we feel with our souls, revealing to us how they express themselves here, in the material world that we share.

Characters

WENDLE   Afro-Canadian, mid twenties
CHRIS   Afro-Canadian, mid twenties
ROBIN   Afro-Canadian, mid twenties
GREG   Afro-Canadian, mid twenties

Setting

WENDLE's luxury warehouse apartment. Front door, wide balcony overlooking Toronto, skylight, basketball net, kitchen with an island, door leading to bedroom, hall leading to bathroom, couch, television, table, desk with computer set up.

Acknowledgements

Special thanks to the Toronto Arts Council, the Ontario Arts Council, Factory Theatre, Canadian Stage Company, National Arts Centre, Layne Coleman, Mom, Dad, Iris Turcott, Katherine Kaszas, Beaner, Tanya, Jay Kaitell, Brent Smyth, Martin Bragg, Ken Gass, David Collins, Marti Maraden, Victoria Steele, Brent Smyth, Mathew Rockall, Randy Hughson, Dave Carley, David Collins, David Abel, Richard Yearwood, Derwin Jordan, Andrew Jason Wade, Conrad Coates, Heather Ann McCallum, Cate Banfield, Rick Rose, Victoria Wallace, Steve Lucas, Marc Desormeaux, Diana Tyndale, Alexandra Lunney, Suzanne Roy, and Cate.

Production Credits

A Common Man's Guide to Loving Women was premiered at the National Arts Centre (Ottawa) and The Canadian Stage Company (Toronto) in a co-production between the NAC and the CSC. The first performance was on March 1, 1999 at the NAC, with the following cast:

WENDLE .... Conrad Coates
CHRIS .... Derwin Jordan
ROBIN .... Andrew Moodie
GREG .... Andrew Jason Wade

Directed by Layne Coleman
Set and costume design by Victoria Wallace
Lighting design by Steve Lucas
Sound design by Marc Desormeaux
Stage Manager: Heather Ann McCallum
Assistant Stage Manager: Cate Banfield
Assistant Director: Rick J. Rose
Assistant Lighting Designer: Sandra Marcroft

A Common Man's Guide to Loving Women was commissioned by the Canadian Stage Company (Toronto) and workshopped by David Collins, Derwin Jordan, Andrew Moodie and Richard Yearwood, directed by Layne Coleman.

Andrew Moodie

Andrew Moodie is an Ottawa-born and raised actor, with extensive stage, film and television credits. *Riot*, his first play (Scirocco, 1997), was an immediate success with critics and audiences after premiering in 1995 at Toronto's Factory Theatre. It was subsequently remounted at the 1996 du Maurier World Stage Festival in Toronto, and produced at Ottawa's Great Canadian Theatre Company, and Halifax's Neptune Theatre. It won the 1996 Chalmers Canadian Play Award. Andrew's second play, *Oui*, premiered at Toronto's Factory Theatre in 1998.

Act One

(At rise: GREG is playing Nintendo. ROBIN is reading a magazine. CHRIS is screaming on the phone with his fiancée.)

GREG: He runs the court, to Jordan, for three...brick. Brick brick brick, just like Damon Stou...

ROBIN: Don't start with me.

GREG: Just like the love of your life—Damon Stoudamire.

ROBIN: He has got the most incredible crossover dribble in the league.

GREG: If he doesn't bounce the ball off his foot.

ROBIN: The quick release off his jumper? You cannot defend against it.

GREG: Unless you put a hand in his face.

ROBIN: Portland Trailblazers, 81 million dollar contract for six years.

GREG: He chokes!

ROBIN: Fuck you man.

(WENDLE walks out of the bedroom with a stack of files and goes towards the computer.)

GREG: When it's money time, he cashes out!

(WENDLE motions as if he's about to say something. He doesn't.)

ROBIN: Okay, maybe he's not a Tim Hardaway or a Turrel Brandon…

GREG: Hey what, sorry?

WENDLE: What?

GREG: I thought you were going to say something.

WENDLE: No no. No.

GREG: I'm not even sayin' it's his fault. But I think he has got to go get some Tim Robbins motivational tapes or something…

WENDLE: You have your cell phone here? Robin?

ROBIN: Yo.

WENDLE: You have your cell phone here?

ROBIN: Naw man. Left it at home.

(WENDLE goes back into the bedroom.)

GREG: Coke, Pepsi, Sprite?

ROBIN: 7-Up.

GREG: Yeah. Me too. Thanks.

(ROBIN stares at GREG, then goes to the kitchen and grabs two cans of pop.)

This game sucks.

ROBIN: Where's Turok?

GREG: You had it last.

ROBIN: I did not.

GREG: You are such a lying bastard.

(WENDLE steps out of the bedroom again, looking through file.)

	Well?
WENDLE:	I think that's it.
GREG:	Oh man.
ROBIN:	That's gotta hurt.
WENDLE:	You guys gonna stick around right?
ROBIN:	Yeah?
GREG:	Oh uh, Wendle?
WENDLE:	What.
GREG:	Can you get an extra ticket for tonight?
WENDLE:	For who?
GREG:	A friend. Friend of mine. Tabitha. Did you ever meet her?
WENDLE:	Well, I'll have to make a call.
GREG:	If it doesn't happen, I will totally understand.
WENDLE:	No, it shouldn't be a problem. It shouldn't be a problem at all.
ROBIN:	Hockey? Hockey?
GREG:	Uh, sure.
ROBIN:	Have I told you how much I love your new digs.
WENDLE:	What?
ROBIN:	This is a great apartment man.
WENDLE:	Yeah, yeah.
ROBIN:	I wanted to get a place in the Candy Factory, but the mothafucka's charging three hundred thousand dallas for a muthafuckin' shoe box.
WENDLE:	I need to use a phone.

GREG: Try next door, maybe the neighbour's?

WENDLE: Right. You'll be here right?

ROBIN: We're not going anywhere.

(WENDLE leaves.)

GREG: Who're you taking?

ROBIN: Senators. What?

GREG: I'm taking the Habs.

ROBIN: Fine.

GREG: And I am going to bludgeon you to death.

ROBIN: In your wet dreams you little girlie man.

CHRIS: *(Offstage.)* I AM LISTENING TO YOU!!! I AM!!!

GREG: You ready?

ROBIN: I gotta set up my lines!

GREG: You think that's going to help?

CHRIS: *(Offstage.)* No no you take a step back! No no, you take a step back!

GREG: It's funny, even with all this going on, I still want to get married.

ROBIN: You want to get married?

GREG: Oh yeah.

ROBIN: Why?

GREG: Well…

ROBIN: Why?

GREG: I'm thinking it's about that time.

ROBIN: To do what?

GREG: Settle down. You know? And that paternal clock thing is ticking louder and louder.

ROBIN: You want a kid?

GREG: I cannot wait to be a father.

ROBIN: What do you want, boy or a girl?

GREG: Boy. Two boys. That's what I want.

ROBIN: No no give me girls man. Girls are great, they're like Daddy's little princess. Boys? Boys are great for about 13 years, then one day, you open the door to their room and they're like; their head's spinning around, eyes are rollin' back in their skull going 'Must Kill Father. Don't know why. Must kill Father.'

GREG: Not my boys.

ROBIN: No not your boys.

(WENDLE returns.)

GREG: Not home?

WENDLE: Yeah.

GREG: Is it about the thing?

WENDLE: Yeah.

(CHRIS walks out of the bedroom.)

CHRIS: The wedding's off.

ROBIN: Get out.

CHRIS: That's it.

WENDLE: Man.

CHRIS: That's it. We're done.

GREG: What happened?

CHRIS: She met somebody.

ROBIN: Aww.

GREG: Tough break man.

CHRIS: Yeah.

ROBIN: Was it another guy or was it a woman?

CHRIS: What?

ROBIN: It was a guy right?

CHRIS: Yeah.

> (ROBIN gives WENDLE and GREG a $10 bill each.)

ROBIN: What the… I thought it was going to be another woman. It's in now.

GREG: So this guy, who is he?

CHRIS: I don't know, some guy she worked with on tour. You really thought she might be lesbian?

ROBIN: I was just hoping, that's all.

WENDLE: So who is this guy, what's his name?

CHRIS: Hughson. Randy Hughson. Some blond-haired, blue-eyed, GQ-looking son of a bitch.

GREG: Is he like a big name actor or something?

CHRIS: Yeah. What?

ROBIN: She's star fucking.

GREG: Big time!

ROBIN: Star fucking.

CHRIS: Think so?

GREG: That's the only way she is going to get her no talent

	ass up to the top.
WENDLE:	I'll just be a second.

(WENDLE goes to the bedroom.)

GREG:	Can I tell you something?
CHRIS:	What?
GREG:	Five words, alright? Get y'self a white woman!
ROBIN:	Mmhmm.
GREG:	Get y'self a white woman! You have done your duty for the race and look where it got you! White women? They are obedient, they know who's boss, they're not up in your face all the time with 'Tell me that you love me tell me that you need me' crap!
ROBIN:	All dat women's lib stuff. Dat dat dat dat dat dat's just for de white man!
GREG:	You show her 18 inches of Alabama black snake…
ROBIN:	You say jump, she will ask you how high!
CHRIS:	Aren't you married to a black woman.

(ROBIN realizes he is, and starts to cry.)

GREG:	Now look what you've gone and done.
ROBIN:	No, it's alright. I'm fine. I'm fine.
GREG:	What are you doing?
CHRIS:	Just going to the store.
ROBIN:	What do you need, we got everything here, pop, chips, what do you want.
CHRIS:	I just want to go the store.
GREG:	I'll go. What do you need?

CHRIS:	It's alright, I'm just going to the store, I'll be back in a second, just get out of my way.	GREG:	What do you want to get at the store, whatever it is, I can get it.

ROBIN: What do you want. What.

CHRIS: Just wanted to get a cigarette.

GREG/
ROBIN: No no no no!

CHRIS: Get out of my way.

ROBIN: Come on man, you've been doing so good!

CHRIS: It's just one cigarette, for crying out loud.

GREG: Just stop, sit for a second.

CHRIS: I don't want to.

ROBIN: Just relax, sit down, let's wait for Wendle to come back, then we can go out, have some dinner.

CHRIS: Actually, I think I might just go home.

GREG/
ROBIN: What are you crazy! Hey, you can't do that!

CHRIS: I want to go home.

GREG: Yo C dis here weekend's fa you bra.

CHRIS: I want to thank you guys but I really can't stay here.

GREG: Alright sit. I want you to sit.

CHRIS: Guys.

ROBIN: Sit ya nigga ass down, aight.

(ROBIN makes CHRIS sit down.)

CHRIS: Alright.

GREG: We are not going to let you go home.

CHRIS: Why?

GREG: This weekend is yours. If you want to chill that's fine, but you are going to have to do it with us.

CHRIS: Am I on a suicide watch or something?

GREG/
ROBIN: No no no no.

ROBIN: You don't want to be alone now, come on, think about it. You should be with your friends.

CHRIS: Look, I appreciate all the concern, that's great, it's inspiring, but I'm handling it. Okay? It's not a big deal. Now if you'll excuse me, I want to head home.

ROBIN: But we, we planned a surprise for you.

CHRIS: I am not in the mood for a stripper.

ROBIN: Okay, then we've got another surprise for you.

CHRIS: What is it?

(ROBIN makes a bunting motion.)

GREG: What.

(ROBIN whispers in GREG's ear. GREG hesitates. ROBIN slaps him and whispers in his ear.)

You remember Tabitha? You know. A month ago, when we met for that movie? She works for this idiot over here.

CHRIS: Oh right, right.

GREG: She's coming to the game, and she wants a post-game beer with you.

CHRIS: Aren't you madly in love with her?

GREG: I'm not in love with her.

ROBIN: She just remembers you from the movie and she wants to get together, beer afterwards, that's all.

CHRIS: I find it hard to believe that she would remember who I am.

GREG: How could she forget a man as intelligent, as scintillating…

ROBIN: Scintillating.

GREG: And ebullient as you are.

ROBIN: Yeah.

CHRIS: Look, I know what you guys are trying to do. You're trying to pull a sacrifice bunt…

GREG/ROBIN: No.

CHRIS: You sacrifice the woman you're going after, to get me on base…

GREG/ROBIN: NO!

CHRIS: Thanks for the offer, you guys go out, have fun, I'm going home.

ROBIN: Hey hey hey HEY! Stop. Now just, come here. Come here. Don't try and pretend that you're not going through stuff right now, alright? Cause it's not…we care about you, and I don't think we'd be good friends if we just let you run away off on your own and tear yourself apart. I couldn't do that. Neither of us could. Now just let us be here for you. Alright? We'll go out, do some stuff together, try and keep your spirits up. Let us do that for you. Alright? Tomorrow night you can do whatever the hell you want to do, but tonight, you belong to us, okay? Alright?

CHRIS: Okay.

ROBIN: What is it?

CHRIS: I'm fine. Back in a second.

(CHRIS goes to the washroom.)

GREG: He's not fine.

ROBIN: Not at all.

(WENDLE enters from the bedroom.)

GREG: Good news?

(WENDLE uses his body to tell them that he doesn't think things are going well but he doesn't want to give up hope. A noise from the bathroom. WENDLE listens.)

WENDLE: How's the kid?

ROBIN: Eeeh.

GREG: Tickets? Did you get the tickets?

WENDLE: Oh for crying out loud.

GREG: If it's a hassle…

WENDLE: No it's not at all, I'm just…let me just call now.

GREG: Seriously, if it's a hassle.

WENDLE: It's not a hassle, don't worry about it.

(WENDLE goes back into the bedroom. CHRIS comes out of the bathroom blowing his nose.)

CHRIS: You know what I just realized?

GREG: What?

CHRIS: I will never have to see another play again.

ROBIN: I thought you loved theatre.

CHRIS: I fucking HATE theatre.

GREG: Then why were you always going?

ROBIN: Because you wanted to be a good boyfriend.

CHRIS: I wanted to be a good boyfriend.

ROBIN: Now you don't have to see a play ever again.

GREG: What was that piece of garbage thing you dragged me to?

ROBIN: You went to see a play?

CHRIS: Some piece of crap.

GREG: Let me tell you something. Next time I step into a theatre, I want to see something blow up, get swept away in a tornado, I wanna see some dinosaur chomping on some little kid's head, knowhamsayin'?

CHRIS: You know what? I am so glad that I am out of this relationship. I am. I am so glad.

GREG: Good.

CHRIS: I was kinda worried there for a second. I thought I was going to feel some kind of like…it's like a weight's gone, you know? It's like this vice has just…

ROBIN: I hear ya.

CHRIS: You know what? Let's go to a strip joint.

ROBIN: Let's have some fun.

CHRIS: I do believe gentlemen, that I am in the mood for a table dance.

GREG: I do believe you are in the mood for a few table dances.

(Enter WENDLE.)

WENDLE: Got the tickets.

GREG:	If it was a hassle.
WENDLE:	It wasn't a hassle, I'm just...y'know?
GREG:	Tadow.
ROBIN:	So what's the plan Stan?
CHRIS:	What time does the game start?
WENDLE:	Eight. I figure we go to Spinnakers, grab a meal, see the game.
GREG:	We were thinking it might be nice instead to have a pre-game beer at, say, Brass Rail, For Your Eyes Only, Zanzibar!
WENDLE:	No peeler bars. Not tonight.
GREG:	Oh great.
WENDLE:	I'm not in the mood. Not tonight.
ROBIN:	They will get you in the mood, that's what they're paid for.
WENDLE:	Look, you go to see these women, who are, well, let's just say, these are women who haven't made the best career choices in life. Right? Then you have the 21 year-old guys screaming like they ain't never seen a naked woman before in their life. Then you got the guys in their fifties sitting alone, sipping their pathetic little beer, thinking to themselves 'Oh she's lookin' at me eh. Oh, she wants me bad eh.' And then you have the table dance. The dancer comes to your table to dance just for you, not because she likes you, not because she gives a damn about you, no, she knows that a man's IQ shrinks in direct proportion with the growth of his erection. By the end of the night, you've got blue balls, and she's got all your money. I mean, why the hell would you want to waste a perfectly good evening doing that?

ROBIN/
GREG/
CHRIS: I don't know. You got me. Sounds alright to me. Gee, you got a point there. I could kinda go for it right now actually.

    (Phone rings.)

WENDLE: Don't answer it.

CHRIS: But it could be...

WENDLE: Well, okay I'll get it. Just...okay.

    (WENDLE goes to his room. GREG smacks ROBIN on the head and points to the Nintendo. As they start playing, CHRIS goes to the kitchen area. On his way he tries to hear what WENDLE is saying.)

GREG: Got your lines?

ROBIN: Got my lines.

GREG: Penalties?

ROBIN: Penalties.

GREG: Welcome to the house of pain.

ROBIN: Welcome ladies and gentlemen to the Corel Centre. Tonight's match, it's the Sens versus the Habs as...

GREG: Just press the damn start button!

ROBIN: Bam!

GREG: Here we go.

CHRIS: Guys.

GREG: Oh you want some of this.

ROBIN: Come here you bastard.

CHRIS: Guys.

ROBIN: Boomshakalak!

GREG: You son of a bitch.

CHRIS: Guys, what's up with Wendle? Guys?

GREG: Damphousse with the wrap around...

ROBIN: He makes the save!

CHRIS: Guys. What's up with Wendle? Come off it guys.

GREG: Tell him.

ROBIN: You tell him.

CHRIS: Tell me what?

GREG: Don't worry about it. Ohhh! That was tripping, right there.

CHRIS: Don't worry about what?

ROBIN: You've got enough on your plate right now. Don't sweat it.

CHRIS: I am going to take that game and beat both of your skulls with it if you don't tell me what the fuck is going on.

GREG/
ROBIN: Ohhhh!

GREG: That's gotta hurt.

ROBIN: Yashin on the breakaway...

GREG: No.

ROBIN: Suck it down muthafuckaaaaaaa...

(CHRIS unplugs the game.)

Aaaaaargh!

GREG: Aah ah ah ah...

ROBIN: Fuck off Chris.

CHRIS: What's going on with Wendle?

ROBIN: Wendle's been fired.

CHRIS: What!

GREG: He hasn't been fired, he might be fired.

CHRIS: Why?

ROBIN: That girl he was seeing? What's her face. She charged him with rape.

CHRIS: What?

GREG: You're not supposed to know.

(ROBIN *plugs the game back in.*)

ROBIN: Come on.

GREG: I don't want to play.

ROBIN: Fuck you, you're playing.

CHRIS: Diane charged him with rape? Guys...

GREG: You're not supposed to know.

CHRIS: Why?

GREG: Because you've got enough stuff to deal with. I don't want to play.

CHRIS: When did this happen?

ROBIN: Couple days ago.

CHRIS: Why didn't somebody call me?

GREG: You had stuff on your plate.

ROBIN: Where's Turok?

(GREG grabs Turok with his feet and tosses it at ROBIN.)

CHRIS: What do you guys think?

ROBIN: Wendle is not a rapist. He can be loud, obnoxious, petty, insulting, he can be a lot of things, but he's not a rapist.

GREG: You should talk to him.

CHRIS: Yeah I should.

GREG: So what do you want to do after the game. Go to a club.

CHRIS: Sure. Whatever.

GREG: I know the bouncers at Joker. Tell them that you work with me at City and I can get you in. No problem.

CHRIS: Sounds good.

GREG: First off, do you have condoms?

CHRIS: No.

GREG: Here.

(He takes some out of his back pocket and gives them to CHRIS.)

CHRIS: Extra large?

GREG: That's what I got. Take it or leave it.

ROBIN: I tried those once and they just fit. I hated that. If I'm gonna wear extra large I want it to be tight you know what I mean?

CHRIS: Too much information.

ROBIN: And they're so thick! I couldn't believe it, it was like wearing a shower cap.

GREG: They're not that thick.

ROBIN: Muthufuckin' garbage bag man.

GREG: Not when it's nice and snug.

CHRIS: Alright, enough all ready.

ROBIN: Is that what you're going to wear?

CHRIS: What's wrong with what I'm wearing?

ROBIN: Do you think he'd fit into one of Wendle's silk shirts?

GREG: Mmmmm.

ROBIN: What about his leather pants.

CHRIS: I am not wearing leather pants.

ROBIN: Okay, so you're dressed up, you're hanging with us and across the room, a sexy, 22 year-old, wearing tight, tight jeans and a form fitting T-shirt starts giving you the eye, you do what.

CHRIS: I…I give up, what.

ROBIN: You ditch us and go talk to her.

CHRIS: No no no.

ROBIN: I can't work with this.

CHRIS: I am not in any shape to pick up chicks tonight.

GREG: Come on guy, you gotta get back on that horse.

CHRIS: Look at me. I am…I'm in no shape to start looking for a relationship.

ROBIN: Who the hell's talking about a relationship, we're trying to get you laid.

GREG: Okay, so she walks by the table and on her way to the washroom, she looks right into your eyes, what do you do?

CHRIS: I…

GREG: You talk to her.

CHRIS: I talk to her.

ROBIN: What do you say?

CHRIS: Hi?

GREG: Hi's good.

CHRIS: Hello.

GREG: Hi, hello, if she's American… Mmm mm MM Get a look at yourself! Girl, you lookin' so good right now, I could sop you up with a biscuit!

ROBIN: Americans love that shit.

GREG: And say it loud.

ROBIN: Americans are loud, very loud.

CHRIS: Right, okay.

GREG: Okay, so, you start talking to her.

ROBIN: She says 'Hi'.

GREG: What do you say?

CHRIS: Uh, so…

(GREG makes a buzzer sound.)

ROBIN: Wrong!

GREG: Never hesitate.

CHRIS: Never?

ROBIN: Hey, how you doing? Having a good time?

GREG: Hi, my name's Chris, what's your name?

ROBIN: You look familiar. Don't you work at that bar around College and Clinton.

CHRIS: I see.

GREG: Go right to her. Don't talk about yourself.

ROBIN: No.

GREG: You want her to feel special, like you want to know more about her.

CHRIS: Ah.

ROBIN: Hey, watch the eyes buster, up I'm up here, not down here.

CHRIS: Sorry.

GREG: So go ahead, ask her something.

CHRIS: But I don't...

(GREG whispers in his ear.)

CHRIS: Did you go to Ryerson?

ROBIN: No. No I didn't.

CHRIS: Oh. Uh sorry.

(GREG makes buzzer noise.)

What!

ROBIN: Right away, you got to get in there right away.

GREG: You look so much like someone I knew from U of T, she was a friend of my sister's.

CHRIS: I don't have a sister.

GREG: You...look...

ROBIN: When you use this approach you communicate that you went to university, maybe you have a good job, nice car.

GREG: Next you want to get her name, and when you get her name...

GREG/
ROBIN: Remember it.

ROBIN: You can't be waking up the next day trying to figure out how the hell you're going to open up her wallet so you can find her driver's licence. That's kinda low class.

CHRIS: Right.

GREG: So talk about her name for a bit, get to know it. Go for it.

ROBIN: Keeping the eyes on the face.

CHRIS: So what's your name?

ROBIN: Shaniqua.

CHRIS: Isn't that an old Afro-American slave name?

GREG: No no no no...

CHRIS: It's a valid question.

ROBIN: Keep going keep going just keep going.

(GREG whispers in his ear.)

CHRIS: So Shaniqua, what do you do for a living?

ROBIN: I'm an assistant to the deputy for Intergovernmental Affairs for the provincial government.

CHRIS: So, do you come here often?

GREG/
ROBIN: OWW!

CHRIS: What!

GREG: He just gave you a beautiful opening!

CHRIS: What!

ROBIN: When a woman tells you her job, especially a big

	important job, chances are she wouldn't mind telling you just a little bit more about it.
GREG:	Stop thinking you, you, you all the time!
ROBIN:	This whole exercise is meant to get her talking about herself.
CHRIS:	Intergovernmental Affairs, wow, what's that?
GREG:	There we go!
ROBIN:	Well right now I'm an assistant to the deputy but I want to move to the Environment portfolio where I can make more of a difference. Besides the deputy is a sexist asshole.
CHRIS:	Men are pigs.
	(GREG gives CHRIS an emphatic thumbs up.)
ROBIN:	Yeah, I know. What do you do?
CHRIS:	I work in a law firm. Corporate law. You know.
ROBIN:	Oh really.
CHRIS:	Right now my job is to go around to corporations and advise them on employment equity, equal pay for women, stuff like that.
	(GREG goes nuts, doing a hockey player "goal" move.)
ROBIN:	Oh really!
CHRIS:	If this guy is a sexist pig I may be able to give you some legal options free of charge.
GREG:	Beautiful!
CHRIS:	That is, if you could show me your legal options on the dance floor.
GREG:	Congratulations Christopher Ewert, you are now officially on base number...

GREG/
ROBIN: One!

CHRIS: I just offered free legal advice as a veiled request for sexual favours.

ROBIN: And it was beautiful.

GREG: Keep that up and you will be knee-deep in booty by ten o'clock.

WENDLE: *(Offstage.)* Fuck you fuck you fuck fuck fuck fuck!

(The guys want to open the door, but feel they can't.)

ROBIN: Eh Wendle. You okay in there? Wendle.

WENDLE: *(Offstage.)* Yeah.

ROBIN: You okay in there.

WENDLE: *(Offstage.)* I'll be out in a second.

(CHRIS pulls out a $20 bill.)

CHRIS: Guys could you do me a favour and go get some chips and crackers and stuff.

(GREG takes the money and heads for the door.)

ROBIN: But I want to play Turok.

GREG: Don't make me bitch slap you.

ROBIN: I mo kick yo ath!!

(They exit repeating their lines. WENDLE enters with the phone.)

WENDLE: Where's Tweedledum and Tweedledumber?

CHRIS: They went out to get some chips and stuff.

WENDLE: Ah. You want to…you want a drink? I've got some Glenlivet here.

CHRIS: No thanks.

WENDLE: Sure?

CHRIS: Yeah.

WENDLE: Do you mind if I...

CHRIS: No no. Go ahead. So who were you screaming at in there.

WENDLE: Nothing. Don't worry about it.

CHRIS: Robin and Greg tell me that you got into a little trouble with Diane?

WENDLE: Yeah.

CHRIS: Want to tell me about it?

WENDLE: This woman...I...we were perfect for each other. Perfect. She even came to church with me. I thought this was the one. I was sure that this was the one. Six months, we went out for six months, no sex.

CHRIS: Really.

WENDLE: We both felt that even though premarital sex is okay, it's just not something you do on a first date, or a second date or, whatever. Anyway, eventually we came to a point when we both decided that it's time, that we need to take the next step.

CHRIS: Right, okay.

WENDLE: So I suggest making it something special, you know? So one day, when we're both not working, go to Toronto Island, go to the park, we have a really expensive meal, we go to a movie, something romantic. And then come back here. I had the place all decked out with candles, rose petals from the door to the bedroom kinda thing...

CHRIS: You went all out.

WENDLE: I went for broke. Cause I wanted this to be something special.

CHRIS: Okay.

WENDLE: So we start, you know...

CHRIS: Yes.

WENDLE: So then, she goes, "Do you have a condom." And uh, I was thinking so much about everything else and, uh, you know, I forgot. I did, I forgot...

CHRIS: So you...

WENDLE: Put my clothes back on, went downstairs, got the condoms, come back up here, put one on, and then we start.

CHRIS: Okay.

WENDLE: Okay, so we're going along there for a while, and I start to notice a burning sensation.

CHRIS: Burning?

WENDLE: Yeah, kinda like if you had an infection, only it was sudden, it was like immediate.

CHRIS: And that was when you had the condom on.

WENDLE: Yeah. Now, I didn't know what was happening at the time, but now I think I might be allergic to the spermicide or something.

CHRIS: Oh come on.

WENDLE: No I'm serious. It hurt. Really bad. I'm serious!

CHRIS: Okay, alright, go ahead.

WENDLE: I'm not fucking around with you, it hurt!

CHRIS: Okay, sure, go on.

(The front door buzzer goes off. The buzzer has a light that flashes. WENDLE gets it.)

WENDLE: Who is it?

ROBIN: (O.S.) Luke, I am your father Luke...

(WENDLE presses the buzzer to let them in.)

WENDLE: Anyway, so, so, and this is where things get fucked up, because, okay, what happened was I took the condom off and went to start again, and she was all like, "I don't know." But I told her, Look, you don't have to worry about me, I have only slept with maybe three other women in my entire life, I don't have any diseases or anything. But she was still like, "I don't know" so we talked for a bit, I think I've convinced her, I start again, and she's just like lying there. I finish and I say look, I'm sorry honey, 'cause I can tell she's mad right. She goes to the end of the bed, starts putting on her clothes. I tell her I'm sorry and she looks at me and says, "You know, you just raped me." I'm like, WHAT! I try to talk to her, she doesn't want to hear it. She's gone. Next day, I'm calling her from work, calling her and calling her, as I'm sitting at my desk, two police officers come up to me, tell me I am under arrest for rape, handcuff me and take me out of the office and right to the Don Jail.

CHRIS: Whoa.

WENDLE: You know what she told the cops, this is what pissed me off the most. You know what she put in her affidavit? Wait, I got it right here, wait. Where is it. Here. She says that I tore off the condom, and with a look on my face of hatred for all women, I brutally raped her. Here, this is the best part: "Once he was finished, he turned to me and said, 'All you white bitches are the same.' And it was then I knew the relationship was over. I knew I didn't want to become another Nicole Simpson."

CHRIS: Let me see this.

WENDLE: By all means.

CHRIS: "We had been dating for a week"?

WENDLE: Yeah, yeah, she's trying to make it sound like we just met or something. And I don't know who the hell she can fool with that because I introduced her to the entire office staff six months ago telling everyone that this is our first date...

(GREG and ROBIN enter. ROBIN jumps on the couch and uses the remote to turn the TV sound off.)

GREG: We have decided that we will go to Insomnia first because...

ROBIN: The waitresses wear tight clothing.

GREG: No, because it is a better environment for you and Tabitha to talk and get to know each other.

WENDLE: Why the hell are you trying to set Chris up with the woman you're in love with.

GREG: I'm not in love with her.

(The phone rings.)

WENDLE: Don't answer it!

CHRIS: But...

WENDLE: Don' t.

CHRIS: But it could be...

ROBIN: Get call display for crying out loud!

(CHRIS answers the phone.)

CHRIS: Hello? Hi. Yeah.

(CHRIS takes the phone cord and waves to WENDLE to help him get the phone into the bedroom.)

Uhm, no. No it's okay. Yeah. Well I don't know.

(CHRIS goes into the bedroom.)

ROBIN:	Beer?
WENDLE:	Sure.
ROBIN:	Ginger ale?
GREG:	Yeah, thanks.
WENDLE:	So tell me about this Tabitha woman. Greg?
GREG:	Yeah?
WENDLE:	How did you meet her?
GREG:	Uh, through Robin.
ROBIN:	She's one of the managers at the store.
WENDLE:	I see.
ROBIN:	He came in one day, looking for an action flick, she astounded him with her acute knowledge of every Jackie Chan film ever made, and the rest, as they say, is history.
WENDLE:	Well, so how does it look?
GREG:	We're just doing the friends thing right now.
WENDLE:	Well, let me tell you—

(He gets a bottle opener and offers it to ROBIN.)

You need an opener? Let me tell you, don't do the dating for six month thing.

ROBIN:	There is nothing wrong with sex on the first date. My wife and I had the most amazing sex on our first date. It was a sign from God.
WENDLE:	You know, in all my years of living on this planet, one thing that never ceases to amaze me, is how a woman can be the source of such incredible pleasure, and such great pain. Great pain. It starts off innocently enough; you spend your teens giggling, and laughing at them. Teasing them.

Dreaming about them. You spend your twenties chasing them into crouched, dark corners of cheap bars, talking bullshit in some form or another. You bust your ass to get the job, to get the apartment, to get the clothes, to get the car, to build the kind of life that some woman, somewhere, is going to share with you someday. Then, after a while, you start to realize that, hey, it just might not happen for me. This idea that someone is out there for you, that there is someone special out there, just for you, is all a load of bullshit. A deep self-delusion propagated by movies, music, TV ads, sitcoms, all forms of print media, and your own mother. All conspiring to hide from you the deep dark truth that...

WENDLE: Gentlemen, I propose a toast. This is not exactly what I saw for myself, not where I thought I would be at this point in my life, but, hey...here I am. Here I am.

(GREG puts his hand on WENDLE's shoulder. CHRIS enters.)

CHRIS: She'll be here in an hour.

WENDLE: Let's go.

CHRIS: No, I want to stay.

GREG: What are you crazy?

CHRIS: She sent me an e-mail, I want to read the e-mail. I want to stay here and meet her.

GREG: Not a good idea.

ROBIN: Are you sure about this?

CHRIS: Yeah, that's what I want to do.

WENDLE: But we'll miss the first ten minutes of the game.

CHRIS: You guys go, go ahead. You don't have to stay here. It's okay. I mean it.

ROBIN: No it's alright.

CHRIS: Go. Go to the game, I'll meet you there.

GREG: We'll stay until she gets here. Then we'll go to the game, okay?

WENDLE: Fine.

CHRIS: You don't have to do this.

WENDLE: Wanna get your e-mail?

CHRIS: Can I use your computer?

WENDLE: Sure.

(WENDLE goes to the computer and turns it on.)

ROBIN: Is this new?

WENDLE: Upgrade.

ROBIN: What do ya got?

WENDLE: Pentium III 500mhz. 32 speed CD ROM, 9 gig hard drive, 128 meg SD RAM, 17 inch monitor with an ATI AGP 12 meg graphics card, ISDN Internet connection.

ROBIN: Can I touch it?

WENDLE: I can have any of the firm's data bases on here and work on it remotely from my laptop anywhere in the world.

GREG: I've got a Mac.

CHRIS: I told her what you said about being a lesbian.

ROBIN: Oh yeah?

CHRIS: She laughed.

ROBIN: Really.

CHRIS: She said all women are bi anyway so you should have won the bet.

ROBIN: Is that what she said?

WENDLE: All women are not bi.

CHRIS: That's what she said.

ROBIN: If I were a woman, I'd be a major lesbian.

GREG: If I woke up one day and discovered I was a woman, I would lock the door, curl up in bed and figure out what the hell the difference is between a vaginal orgasm and a clitoral orgasm.

ROBIN: Tadow.

WENDLE: This whole lesbian thing, I don't get it.

GREG: You don't get it?

WENDLE: I just don't get it.

ROBIN: You don't find the lesbian thing a turn on?

WENDLE: Chris, you want to enter your e-mail password?

CHRIS: Sure.

(CHRIS sits at the computer.)

WENDLE: I don't see how two women…how is that a turn on?

GREG: What is it about two women that turns you off?

WENDLE: Well, it's…but there's no man there. I don't have anything against homosexuals, they were put on this earth with the rest of us and we can all live in harmony and all that shit, but, a woman was made for a man. How can you get so excited about something that's so…so…

ROBIN: So let me get this straight, if you were a woman, you would fuck men, only men and that's it.

WENDLE: Yeah.

ROBIN: Would you fuck me? Would you baby? Come on…

(ROBIN starts caressing WENDLE.)

WENDLE: Fuck off.

ROBIN: I'll rock your world baby.

WENDLE: I'll rock YOUR world—

CHRIS: How do you work the printer?

GREG: Oh my god, Tabitha. Do you have her number?

ROBIN: Where's the phone?

GREG: Let me call her.

(ROBIN and GREG go to the bedroom.)

ROBIN: She's my employee, and I don't care how much you're in love with her.

GREG: I'm not in love with her!

(They enter the bedroom.)

WENDLE: If anybody calls while you're on the phone, I'm not here!

CHRIS: Who are you avoiding?

WENDLE: Some bitch from Human Resources. She's trying to force me out. Thing is, I'm the Director of Finances. My superior is the VP and he thinks this whole thing is bullshit. He gave me my lawyer and thinks I should fight it.

CHRIS: What is she saying?

WENDLE: She knows that the President feels that even though it's a bullshit charge, it could reflect poorly on the firm. The Raptors, they're our biggest client. "DIRECTOR OF FINANCES OF TORONTO MARKETING FIRM RAPES CHEERLEADER". If the papers get a hold of this thing you may as well put a bullet in my head.

CHRIS: So what do they want to do?

WENDLE: They want to suspend me. They don't have a valid reason to suspend me so she's going over all of my shit. Everything. Trying to find some little thing that could give them a reason to suspend the mad rapist.

CHRIS: But I mean, this is not a rape case.

WENDLE: Really?

CHRIS: Well, it's clear that she consented to the original sexual contact, the hospital could not provide any evidence of physical harm, there's no bruises, no evidence of force, and there was already a case very similar to this here in Toronto not too long ago, a precedent has been set. It's not a rape case.

WENDLE: Would you please try my case for me?

CHRIS: What about your lawyer, what does he say?

WENDLE: He thinks I should fight the rape charge.

CHRIS: Really? Has he read this affidavit?

WENDLE: Yeah. What.

CHRIS: What area of law does he practice?

WENDLE: I'm not sure what it's called but he usually does contracts for athletes.

CHRIS: He's way out of his league. He is way out of his element.

WENDLE: Would you try my case for me. Please?

CHRIS: Well, if I were to try your case, I would present the judge with a guilty plea for sexual assault.

WENDLE: You think I raped her.

CHRIS: No.

WENDLE: You think I'm lying.

CHRIS: I think that even with what you told me, an assault occurred.

WENDLE: But I didn't do anything!

CHRIS: In the eyes of the law, you willfully continued intercourse when you knew you had broken the terms of consent.

WENDLE: But we talked about it—

CHRIS: No, *you* talked about it. If she didn't change the rules of consent, then you committed an offense.

WENDLE: But she did!

CHRIS: What did she say? What did she do? If she did, why would she run to the police.

WENDLE: Fuck you.

CHRIS: Wendle, I feel for your position, I do, but if I were to try this case, I would enter a guilty plea for sexual assault. Hey. I'm just telling you what I would tell any prospective client.

WENDLE: They're going to fire me Chris! If I can't beat this thing, they are going to fire me. That's it. Everything gone. All this, everything. Gone.

CHRIS: Well, but, it's it's the law. There's nothing I can do about it. Where are you going?

WENDLE: Out.

CHRIS: Come on man, just, Wendle? Wendle...

(*WENDLE leaves. The printer beeps.*)

End of ACT ONE.

Act Two

(GREG and CHRIS sitting are around, GREG reading Details *magazine, CHRIS skimming over his e-mail. He has already read it. ROBIN is taking shots at the net.)*

GREG: Okay, then what is it that you love the most about your wife?

ROBIN: *(He thinks about it for a while.)* Her intellect.

GREG: Yeah, yeah…

ROBIN: I love that we can debate, and argue ideas, from a place of complete mutual respect. I love that. And we have very different tastes you know? She's always trying to get me to read, some Toni Morrison novel. I'm always dragging her to some West African film at the Film Festival. And so it's like we're constantly challenging each other, you know? I couldn't live without that. I couldn't.

GREG: She's pretty stacked too.

ROBIN: She's got great tits.

GREG: They are beautiful.

ROBIN: You know what else I love about my wife?

GREG: What.

ROBIN: Her clitoris.

GREG: Okay time. Time out. Time.

ROBIN: I am addicted to her clitoris.

GREG: Nonono.

ROBIN: It's so beautiful and soft and—

GREG: Okay thank you, thank you very much.

ROBIN: It's not so small that it's not existent, not so big that it's like another dick, you know what I'm saying?

CHRIS: Whatserface? My former fiancée? She wouldn't let me go down on her.

ROBIN: What!

CHRIS: She told me that it just made her feel uncomfortable.

ROBIN: I am sorry, but if I get a thrill out of licking you into orgasm, give me ten minutes of your day. Hell, make it 20.

GREG: But Chris, were you fresh shaven?

CHRIS: I...I don't know.

GREG: It's a pretty sensitive area down there and if you're rooting around with two days' growth well, imagine a woman jerking you off with a glove made out of wool.

CHRIS: Right, right.

(Pause.)

ROBIN: So is that it, with the quiz, is it over?

GREG: Okay, uhm, how often do you give your wife an orgasm. Every time, more often than not, or don't give a damn.

ROBIN: I think I give her an orgasm every time. I think.

CHRIS: You don't know.

ROBIN: I work hard man. I don't know. I hope so.

GREG: Either she has the orgasm, or she doesn't. What will it be.

ROBIN: She has them, they're just not...she's subtle.

CHRIS: She's not thrashing around, pounding the walls or anything...

ROBIN: Yeah.

GREG: Maybe what you think is a subtle orgasm, is for her, an earth-shattering, mind-expanding, rocket to the moon.

CHRIS: And maybe you're just a really shitty lover.

ROBIN: Hey, look, I'm no genius in the bedroom, but I can mix it up in the corners, I can stickhandle pretty good, and every now and then, I get the puck in the net.

GREG: Remember Crystal? She ejaculated.

CHRIS: I'm sorry?

GREG: She ejaculated. When she came, she would ejaculate.

ROBIN: No fuckin' way.

CHRIS: Did she have a penis?

GREG: No she didn't have a penis.

ROBIN: You've never heard of that?

CHRIS: I have never heard of that.

ROBIN: You've never heard of that!

CHRIS: I have never heard of that.

ROBIN: Oh fuck off.

CHRIS: I have never ever, ever, heard of a woman ejaculating.

GREG: Okay, this is how it would go. We'd be going along there, everything's fine, then whoomp, she clamps down.

CHRIS: She clamps down?

GREG: And starts to squeeze.

CHRIS: Okay...

GREG: It gets tighter, and tighter, and tighter, then she grabs the bed, tells me to shove it in as far as I can, which is pretty far. I push push push push, then boom, it contracts, I get shoved out, her eyes roll back into her skull, and she shoots.

CHRIS: Yeah?

GREG: All over the bed.

ROBIN: She's thrashing around?

GREG: Loses her mind. Two minutes. Loses her mind.

(Pause.)

ROBIN: What does it look like?

GREG: It's clear, it's kinda filmy...

CHRIS: It's not piss is it?

GREG: No no, it's...well, I don't know what it is, but...

ROBIN: I bet you felt like king of the fucking hill.

GREG: Well, at first it was great, but then...

CHRIS: What?

GREG: Well, after a while, it became all about her orgasm. Know what I'm saying? The tenderness started to disappear. Sometimes I felt like a big human dildo.

A lot of times she'd finish way before me, and that doesn't bother me, but then, don't just roll over and fall asleep, right? We can talk, we can hold each other...

CHRIS: You sure she wasn't a guy.

ROBIN: Hey. Quake. Cool.

(He starts playing the computer game.)

CHRIS: Could you turn the sound down please.

(He does.)

GREG: She's not coming man.

CHRIS: You don't think so?

GREG: She was supposed to be here 45 minutes ago.

CHRIS: Well, let's give it ten more minutes.

GREG: She screwing up my friend. Big time. You don't do this to somebody.

CHRIS: I bet this Randy guy knows how to give a woman a mind-blowing orgasm. I bet he is a fucking incredible fucking lover, with a huge dong, and a tongue that just doesn't quit. I bet they're doing it right now. That's what happened. She was heading out the door, then Randy grabbed her by the waist, shattered her will with his sparkling blue eyes, and she couldn't help but ejaculate all over the place. They are swimming in her ejaculate. They are swimming, and making love, they are without a care in the world.

GREG: You know what I am going to do for you? I am going to call up Paula. She's my boss. You'll love her. And maybe she can get her friend Andrea to come along. Not only will they provide much-needed female companionship, but it is much easier to pick up women, if you are surrounded by other women.

CHRIS: Really?

ROBIN: It's like a wedding ring. They love the challenge.

CHRIS: Right.

GREG: I'm going to get you so...

(The door buzzer goes off. They all look at each other. CHRIS goes to the buzzer. It is buzzing frantically. CHRIS answers it.)

CHRIS: I knew you'd show up.

WENDLE: *(Offstage.)* It's me. I forgot my keys.

(CHRIS buzzes him in. GREG and ROBIN chuckle.)

ROBIN: I thought for sure he went to the game without us.

CHRIS: Maybe he did.

GREG: Naw, it's not over yet. He would have stayed for the whole thing.

ROBIN: She's not coming man.

GREG: Come on. We'll go to Insomnia, meet Tabitha. We'll go to Joker, do some dancing, Bob's your uncle.

CHRIS: Tell me more about Tabitha. Who is she, where did you meet her.

GREG: There's nothing to tell man. Come on. Let's go.

CHRIS: Does she know that you're in love with her?

GREG: I'm not...in...go to hell.

ROBIN: So did you and Wendle talk at all?

CHRIS: Yes we did.

ROBIN: You gonna help him out?

CHRIS:	No I don't think so.
ROBIN:	Is there a conflict of interest problem or…
CHRIS:	No. No no.
ROBIN:	It wouldn't affect your job or anything.
CHRIS:	No, not at all.
ROBIN:	Then what's—
CHRIS:	Guys, I hate to…this is my job right? And when a close personal friend asks me to do some legal favour for them, I treat that friend with the same professional standards that I treat anyone. My advice to him was; if I took the case, I would ask him to plead guilty to sexual assault.
ROBIN:	You think he's guilty?
CHRIS:	I know you guys want to help, but you have to let him go out and find other representation.
ROBIN:	S'You want him to say that he raped her?
CHRIS:	I don't want anything, a precedent has been set, there is nothing I can do.
GREG:	But he talked to her.
CHRIS:	Did she say the words; "I give you consent to have sex with me without a condom."?
GREG/ROBIN:	Awwwww come on.
CHRIS:	Did she say the words?
GREG:	Okay, so let's say for a second that she said go for it; sex without a condom. But then right before he's about to come she says I do not give you consent to come inside me.
CHRIS:	Then you have to pull out.

GREG/ ROBIN:	Right! Yeah, Whatever.
CHRIS:	As far as the law is concerned, you have to pull out.
ROBIN:	You can't regulate sex Chris! You can't micro-legislate what two people do in bed together, it's impossible.
CHRIS:	That's the law.
ROBIN:	Okay, let me tell you something: when my wife and I were first…when we started going out, she came with me to visit my Dad in Windsor. So, we're in the rec room in the basement, Dad's upstairs, he's gone to bed, I start groping her, she says 'I don't want to do it in your Dad's house. I say sure fine whatever, I stop. She starts spooning into me. I start again, I get some of her clothes off, she says she's worried that he'll hear us or something, I tell her that the walls are soundproof (they weren't but hey). She says no again, fine, I stop. Then she starts kissing me and…getting me going right? Eventually we're naked, we are doing everything but. So I try again. This time, she doesn't say anything. Okay? So we're going at it, quietly, she is putting my hand on her mouth to stop her from moaning, we finish, we fall asleep, and that's it. Not once did she ever tell me that I had consent to have sex with her. Not once! She could have gone to a police officer the next day and said, "I told him No twice, but he took my clothes off, forced himself into me, he put his hand over my mouth to stop me from making a sound." And I would have to say, "That's exactly what happened."
CHRIS:	But she didn't. She didn't go to the police because whatever it was you two were doing, she consented to. Women do not go through the tests and the photographs and the legal hassle and the possible media attention for fun.

ROBIN: Okay, okay, look.

CHRIS: What.

ROBIN: You see that computer over there? You see this couch, that TV? I don't know anything about her situation, but what if? Okay? What if! The credit cards are maxed out, the rent is five months past due, you owe the tax man, you owe the cable company. I don't know how much those cheerleaders are getting paid, but it ain't this much fucking money! Alright!

CHRIS: I want you to sit down and listen to me for a moment. I never told you guys this, but I had to threaten the firm I'm working for right now with a lawsuit before they would hire me. I had done the interviews, I was told it looked good, I was brought in to see my desk. First day of work I meet the partners. The next day I get a call that I wasn't to come to work, they didn't need me that day. I asked them when they would need me. They told me in about six months. I asked if I was to be paid while I waited for them to need me. They told me no, I wasn't. What do I do? I asked a lawyer to send a little letter informing the firm of Anderson, Johnson and Wade that I would be suing them for a fuck of a lot of money for breach of contract. Well, within two days, I was at my desk. Turns out there was a bit of a power struggle going on. Wade didn't like the idea of someone of my complexion around the office. He, and I quote, "Didn't think I would feel comfortable in that environment." My first day on the job, and they have a whole new department for me. The Department of Equity, that I was to set up and run. It would keep me out of their hair while they did the important business. At first I was real angry, until I realized that I was the one with the most important job in the entire firm. I go around to corporations and give them advice on policies dealing with racial and gender equity. I give seminars. I give one-on-one consultations. I have had a CEO tell me that he will never have a Jew working in his firm. We are about to enter a new century, a new millennium, and there are places that you can't work because you are Jewish? I have had a VP scream at me for two hours that racial equity is a code word for discrimination against the white man. He spent a half an hour trying to convince me that every office tower on Bay street is overrun with Natives and Asians and Blacks. And I have had to explain to a co-worker, a friend of mine, that telling jokes about fucking women until their skulls cave in, is not appropriate for a workplace with a large number of female employees. I know this stuff okay. This is my job. It's what I do. And I am very good at what I do. And I am going to give you something from one of my seminars absolutely free of charge. Now I know this may be hard for you to understand right now, but women have a right to control what happens to their bodies. Period. End of story. I know you guys mean well, and I feel for your position, I do, but if Wendle wants my help it's gonna have to be on my terms.

(WENDLE enters.)

GREG: Where the hell have you been?!

WENDLE: Looking for a fucking lawyer. Any calls for me?

(GREG and ROBIN shake their heads.)

WENDLE: Great. Now everybody get the fuck out of my house.

CHRIS: I'm just going to go downstairs for a second.

(CHRIS leaves.)

WENDLE: Good, now you two, get the fuck out of my house.

ROBIN: Come here. Come.

Andrew Moodie 57

WENDLE: I ain't coming any-fuckin'-where, you are gonna get the fuck out of my house.

GREG: Wendle, now... I want you to listen to me for a second. Now, I am totally on your side, alright? But let's just say hypothetically that maybe you're taking the wrong approach on this thing. Now just hear me out. I'm on your side alright! I am. But I want you to try and step into her frame of mind for a second. She's fine with the whole sex thing, but when you take the condom off, well, maybe she forgot to take the Pill that day, right? Just wait a second. Maybe she did, right? And think about this now, from her perspective, I've known this guy for what, six months? I don' know if he...could he possibly give me something that could...

WENDLE: Wait wait wait. Right there, okay? Right there, okay? Stop. Now. There are a lot of things that I do, that really challenge my relationship with my Creator. I curse like a sailor, the pastor at my church, I can't stand him, think he's a jerk. I am not exactly a poster boy for charity and Christian understanding. I'm not proud of it, but there it is. One of the things that I would never do, EVER, is to knowingly cause physical pain or suffering to someone. Anyone. That's the truth. For me to say anything else, well I...I just can't do that. I can't. I will fight this case with the lawyer I have and God will decide my fate as he always does.

GREG: The truth is very important to you isn't it.

WENDLE: You're damn right it's important.

GREG: Alright. So, the people outside the situation are looking at it, trying to figure out what the truth is. The two people that it happened to are trying to figure out what the truth is. And you know what, it doesn't matter.

WENDLE: The truth doesn't matter.

GREG: It doesn't matter. What matters is dealing with the consequences.

WENDLE: What are you saying.

GREG: The first time that a bully called you a name in the schoolyard, and beat you up. What did your Mom do.

WENDLE: She called the school, she called the kid's parents, called my teacher.

GREG: Right. Now, what did your Dad do?

WENDLE: He said the left is for defence, this right one is the one you hit with.

GREG: Exactly! So the next day you went to school and...

WENDLE: I kicked his ass.

GREG: Yes you did. That's right. Now, if you got caught, would your Dad want you to scream and cry and say it was all his fault?

WENDLE: No.

GREG: No he wouldn't. He would want you to stand up straight. Admit exactly what you did, everything, and face the consequences.

WENDLE: But I didn't hit her.

GREG: No you didn't.

WENDLE: You're trying to say that I hit her?

GREG: No no, all I'm saying is that sometimes, we do things and we think they're okay but they're not okay. And we find out it's not okay, we have to take responsibility for it.

(WENDLE looks at GREG. Looks out the window.)

Wendle?

(WENDLE goes to his bedroom.)

ROBIN: The fuck are you doing telling him he has to plead guilty.

GREG: I'm not saying he has to plead guilty, I just think he's got to say what Chris wants to hear.

ROBIN: Fuck Chris! He's being a fucking asshole.

GREG: Lower your voice.

ROBIN: I know that women have a right to control what happens to their bodies. I know that fuckhead! This is Wendle we're talking about! Wendle. I mean, he could get fired!

GREG: I just think he should start saying what Chris wants to hear.

ROBIN: Is he a rapist?

GREG: No, but, I'm thinking that after six months, his body is a little bit a head of him, if you know what I'm saying.

ROBIN: Did he rape her?!

GREG: No, but I think that it was wrong for him to continue.

ROBIN: Did she try to get up? Did she try to get away? All she had to do was get up. That's it. Get up, put her clothes on.

GREG: Calm down.

ROBIN: And what's all this shit about Nicole Simpson. I mean THAT you know exactly why she said that. You know EXACTLY why she put that in here. Wendle doesn't stand a fucking CHANCE!

GREG: Just shhh, hey…

ROBIN: I am so fucking angry right now!

GREG: Calm down.

ROBIN: Doesn't he see that?

GREG: Just lower your voice.

ROBIN: This is his life! This is his life we're talking about here!

GREG: Look, this is what we're going to do. I have to make a phone call. When Chris gets here, you talk to him, see if there is any legal way we can protect Wendle's job, listen to me, Robin, if this goes down that he has to plead guilty, we need to know if we can protect Wendle's job.

ROBIN: I don't want to talk to Chris right now.

GREG: Yes you are going to talk to Chris, and yes you are going to find out if we can save his job.

ROBIN: I am telling you, I don't think that it's a good idea that I talk to—

(CHRIS enters.)

CHRIS: You know what? I don't think she's coming.

GREG: You got something for me?

CHRIS: I beg your pardon?

GREG: You got something for me?

CHRIS: No.

GREG: Alright. Alright.

CHRIS: What?

(GREG encourages CHRIS to lift his arms. He does. GREG frisks CHRIS and pulls out a pack of cigarettes from his back pocket.)

Hey, stop, hey.

GREG: What the hell is this?

CHRIS: Alright.

GREG: I...I don't know what to say.

CHRIS: I just had one.

GREG: You had three.

CHRIS: Alright fine. Take them. I don't care. I just wanted one.

GREG: It's the devil's weed man! It's the devil's weed!

CHRIS: Fine, fine. Whatever fine.

GREG: I am going to go downstairs, I am going to make a couple of calls. I am going to the corner store, and I am going to give these back to Mr. Pong. And I am going to tell him to never sell you a cigarette ever again!!! I'm not joking!

(GREG goes.)

CHRIS: So do you think he's got a chance with this Tabitha woman?

ROBIN: She's leaving in two weeks.

CHRIS: Ah.

ROBIN: Going to Korea to teach English. For good. She just wants a meaningless roll in the hay before she goes. She hasn't told him yet.

CHRIS: I see. You going to tell him?

ROBIN: She wants me to tell him.

CHRIS: You gonna tell him?

ROBIN: Well, she wants me to tell him.

CHRIS: That's a tough one.

ROBIN: Yes it is. So you think Wendle's guilty of sexual assault.

CHRIS: It's not about what I think. There was a case like this just a few years ago. A precedent has been set. There's nothing I can do about it.

ROBIN: You read the affidavit.

CHRIS: Yes I did.

ROBIN: Come on.

CHRIS: What.

ROBIN: Come on.

CHRIS: What?

ROBIN: "All you white bitches are the same." The same what? It doesn't make any sense. It sounds like something you would put in someone's mouth to make them sound like a monster!

CHRIS: Well, that's what she said happened.

ROBIN: Women are capable of lying Chris.

(In CHRIS' speech, ROBIN echoes "a bit":)

CHRIS: Look, it's obvious that she is embellishing the truth a bit to because she is thinking that she has to plead her case in a justice system run by men.

ROBIN: So we are supposed to allow someone to embellish the truth, because the justice system is run by men?

CHRIS: There are still some judges out there that may not understand that she has a right to control what happens to her own body.

ROBIN: But she had control. She may not have thought she had control but she had control.

CHRIS: But she says that she didn't feel that she did.

ROBIN: Who is responsible for that misunderstanding.

CHRIS: He is.

ROBIN: How is he to know that his intentions are being misunderstood?

CHRIS: He has to check.

ROBIN: Women are not children Chris!

CHRIS: I know.

ROBIN: Sometimes women chose to not say anything and continue because it's just less of a hassle, it's not that she's afraid she'll be brutalized, it's just less of a hassle than to say no and go through having to explain all her contradictory feelings and...

CHRIS: I can't win a case by saying to a judge that she just didn't want the hassle of saying no! That's not good enough!

ROBIN: But if you...

CHRIS: Whoever the judge is, he or she is not going to care who Wendle is, a judge is not going to care that he's your best friend. They're not! They are not going to give a fuck. They are going to care about upholding the law!

ROBIN: Yes but...

CHRIS: Do you have any idea how many women are assaulted every day. And I'm not just talking about the cases we hear about in the newspapers. Everyday...

ROBIN: Yes I know...

CHRIS: Women are being raped, beaten, murdered. A judge is going to say do you have any idea how many women come here.

ROBIN: My wife is more at risk of being attacked by me then anyone else on the planet, I know.

CHRIS: A judge is going to tell you, you have no idea what that's like.

ROBIN: Yes I know what it's like! Yes. Yes I know what it's like for someone to over power you. To take advantage of you. Yes I know what it's like! And I wasn't a 24 year-old woman, I was a nine-year-old boy. I know what it is like for someone to smash your head against a wall because you're screaming, and you're scared. I know what it's like to reach down into a pile of rotting fetid garbage and place your bloody clothing and hide it at the bottom and pray to God that no one ever looks there. I know what that's like. I know what it is like for someone to make you feel like, if you tell anybody, they will kill you. They'll kill you. I know what that's like! My parents, my mother gets sick suddenly, appendicitis, while my dad is at work they put me, the couple down the street, they take care of me. Their kid, he's what, 18? Sadistic fuck who, I knew him from...I...it doesn't matter anyway...

CHRIS: I...

ROBIN: Years later. I'm 16 right? I'm freaking out a bit, feeling like I want to hurt myself or something. It's late at night, I go to this late night rape crisis centre that's open till like ten. I go in there, knock on the door and they tell me that they don't have anyone that can counsel men, they don't. That they don't have any idea where I could go to get counselling, and frankly, they get kinda freaked when some guy is banging on their door at ten o'clock at night and could I kindly leave. And I understood. I did. It didn't make me angry or anything. I just...didn't have anywhere to go.

(He breaks down.)

CHRIS: I didn't know.

ROBIN: No of course you didn't know. Nobody fucking

knows except my wife and the guy that did it. And you can't tell this to Wendle or Greg, right? I didn't tell you this because I want sympathy, or healing or anything. I just, if you take what this woman has said, and treat it as the same thing that, I mean, if you can compare what happened to her, to what happened to me, well, then, fine. But don't ever speak to me again. Ever.

CHRIS: Hey.

ROBIN: I'm alright.

(CHRIS puts his hand on ROBIN's shoulder.)

Don't touch me. I'm alright.

CHRIS: You sure?

ROBIN: I'm fine about it. I am. Really. I know it doesn't look it, but, I can deal with it.

CHRIS: Yeah?

ROBIN: Everybody has something that, you start talking about it, you get a bit of mist in your eyes, but, I am dealing with it. My wife has been a saint. I wouldn't be alive if it wasn't for her. I wouldn't be here.

CHRIS: Alright.

ROBIN: How're you feeling?

CHRIS: I feel stupid, I feel like the stupidest fucking human being on the planet, and, it's like my brain is on fire.

ROBIN: Are you getting that headachy feeling?

CHRIS: It's not a headache. No. It's like my brain is on fire.

ROBIN: Right, right.

CHRIS: It's a slow burning...

ROBIN: You know what's good for that?

CHRIS: What?

ROBIN: Vodka.

CHRIS: Make it a double.

(ROBIN pours drinks.)

What are you thinking? Say it.

CHRIS: That if, I don't know, maybe if I had just loved her the way she needed to be loved.

ROBIN: Don't think that. It's not true. Don't think that way.

CHRIS: But that's what she says in the e-mail.

ROBIN: Well wait now. Think about this one; she's the one who screwed up. She's the one who ran off with another man, and you feel guilty? For what!

CHRIS: Yeah, wait a second.

ROBIN: She's the one who called the wedding off.

CHRIS: That's right.

ROBIN: She's the one who is ending a six year relationship.

CHRIS: Seven and a half.

ROBIN: She's the one who had an affair.

CHRIS: Affairs.

ROBIN: What?

CHRIS: This is her second affair. It was early in the relationship. It was with another woman. She wanted to be sure she wasn't...you know. What?

ROBIN: Chris, okay, I know why you fell in love with her. We all know why you fell in love with her. She is gorgeous. Right? She has an incredible body, she's talented, when she talks to you, she makes you feel

	like you're the most special person in the world, but she's a flake. A major flake.
CHRIS:	You know what you were saying about everyone has one thing that makes you teary-eyed? She had about five. She would have these periods of stability, and then she would just spin and spin. Spin off into space. I thought,we have broken through a lot of stuff, but, I guess we haven't.
ROBIN:	Hey, well, now it's all on this Randy guy. I hope he can handle her.
CHRIS:	I'm such a fucking idiot.
ROBIN:	You're not an idiot.
CHRIS:	I just wish it was me having the affair. That's what pisses me off the most. Why couldn't I have been the one to press the escape button. You know?
ROBIN:	Been there.
CHRIS:	I wish someone had been honest with me and clubbed me over the head or something. I wish someone had just told me look, you're being an idiot, get out, run, have an affair, run away, do what ever. Just dump her.
ROBIN:	So it's over.
CHRIS:	Big time.
ROBIN:	You're not, if she comes in here, you're not going to do something stupid like get back together or nothing.
CHRIS:	No. No. That's it. That's it for me. I'm out.
ROBIN:	Really?
CHRIS:	Actually, at this point, I just want to know if she has the nerve to show up at all.
ROBIN:	Chris.

CHRIS: What?

ROBIN: Chris?

CHRIS: What is it. What.

ROBIN: Remember last New Year's Eve? You were in Calgary.

CHRIS: What.

ROBIN: She came on to me. Nothing happened. Nothing happened. My wife, you can talk to her about it, she was right there. Nothing happened. Actually, she wanted us both to. It's not important, nothing happened.

(GREG enters.)

GREG: Get yourself ready to party tonight. Paula has VIP cards for The Left Bank. She can get us in NO PROBLEM.

(WENDLE enters.)

ROBIN: What's the Left Bank. What's it like?

GREG: The Left Bank. Very chi-chi. Very shoo shoo. I just have to give Tabitha a call before we head out the door.

WENDLE: I am not going anywhere, you guys go out. I mean it. Have a good time.

ROBIN: If we are going to be entertaining these ladies in this apartment later on this evening, we may need some mix.

GREG: I think we have plenty of right, we have to get some mix.

(GREG and ROBIN leave.)

WENDLE: Hey.

CHRIS: Hey.

WENDLE: Look, you want to sit for a second. I want to say something.

CHRIS: You say something, then I say something.

WENDLE: Alright. When she was walking out the door, at the elevator, I yelled at her. I said something hurtful. The exact words of what I said was, "You're just like all the other bitches." It was a terrible hurtful thing to say, but…I thought we had a trust, I…I have been wanting so long to share my life with someone. There were things that happened that night, that I am not proud of. I admit that. I think that men experience love more physically. It's more painful or something. Anyway. There you have it.

CHRIS: When you went to the station, they gave you the HIV test right?

WENDLE: Yeah.

CHRIS: Ever been tested for HIV before?

WENDLE: No. Why?

CHRIS: What we are going to do; Monday, we go to your office, we're going to tell them to cease and desist with the witch hunt. You have been charged with a crime, not convicted of one. We are going to see if we can get some time off for you. So that you can chill out a bit. We wait for the results of the test, then we go on from there.

WENDLE: You're saying she may have given me AIDS?

CHRIS: No, no, no. Wendle, it's standard procedure. As your lawyer, these are things I am supposed to tell you. Before I can do anything, there is a whole slew of bits of information that we both have to know so that I can give this case the best that I am capable of.

WENDLE: She didn't give me AIDS. I feel fine.

CHRIS: There are no symptoms for HIV man.

WENDLE: You think she may have done that to me?

CHRIS: No, no, calm down Wendle you're fine. Don't freak out. All I am saying is that if I am going to take this case, I need to know a whole lot of information. Once I know the information, then I can give you counsel.

WENDLE: Right right.

CHRIS: Hey, hey. hey, Wendle I'm on the case.

WENDLE: Great. Great. Yeah. You know, I have been feeling kinda fluey lately.

CHRIS: Wendle, I am looking after your best interests. Okay?

WENDLE: Alright.

(GREG and ROBIN come back.)

GREG: Guys, come on. Time to go. The girls are going to be there any minute now. And you have to meet my favourite boss, Paula.

CHRIS: Do I?

ROBIN: Paula. City-TV mogul. Intelligent, opinionated, beautiful body. She may be able to get you in free to the Film Festival shindig later on this year.

GEG: You play your cards right my friend and you won't even remember that whatserface ever existed.

ROBIN: Designated driver.

(ROBIN tosses GREG his keys. GREG offers WENDLE his jacket. WENDLE accepts.)

CHRIS: Are you going to bring the car out front?

ROBIN: No! We are leaving through the garage, we are not

going by the front door. If we happen to see any thing that looks like a former fiancée we are driving right past it. Have I made myself clear soldier?

CHRIS: Clear, sir.

GREG: I gotta take a quick whiz!

(GREG runs to the bathroom.)

WENDLE: I'll get the elevator.

(CHRIS pulls out one of the condoms that GREG gave him.)

CHRIS: Here.

WENDLE: No, no thanks.

CHRIS: Oh that's right. You couldn't use these anyway. They're extra large.

WENDLE: Oh, well, in that case.

CHRIS: You know, we've all seen you in your Speedos.

WENDLE: I'm a grow-er, not a show-er.

(WENDLE leaves.)

ROBIN: So you two worked things out?

CHRIS: Yeah.

ROBIN: Cool.

CHRIS: Hey.

(CHRIS goes to hug ROBIN. ROBIN puts out his hand but CHRIS pulls him close and hugs him.)

ROBIN: Alright. Okay.

CHRIS: I'm just giving you a hug for fuck's sake.

ROBIN: It starts with a hug, then we're tellin' each other

	how much we mean to each other, next thing you know, we're sucking each other off.
CHRIS:	Hard to explain to the wife.
ROBIN:	Exactly. Yo Greg! Hurry up!
	(A flush. GREG enters, singing a made-up James Brownesque song. The line below is a suggestion of what it could be.)
GREG:	Hey, good gawd! Sex machine! Heeey! Baby baby baby, baby baby baby!
	(He leaps out the door.)
CHRIS:	You got to tell him.
ROBIN:	I'm going to tell him.
CHRIS:	You got to tell him.
ROBIN:	You want to tell him, you tell him.
CHRIS:	I don't want to tell him. You tell him.
ROBIN:	You can tell him if you want to tell him.
CHRIS:	I ain't gonna tell him, so you better tell him.

(They turn off the lights and leave.

The End.)